FALL LEAVES

COLORING BOOK

This book is printed on just one side of the paper
to avoid bleed through.

To view samples of these illustrations colored by the author please visit
www.lovelyleisure.me

LOVELY LEISURE

ILLUSTRATIONS BY PAULA PARRISH

Fall Leaves Coloring Book
© 2015 Paula Parrish

www.lovely-leisure.com

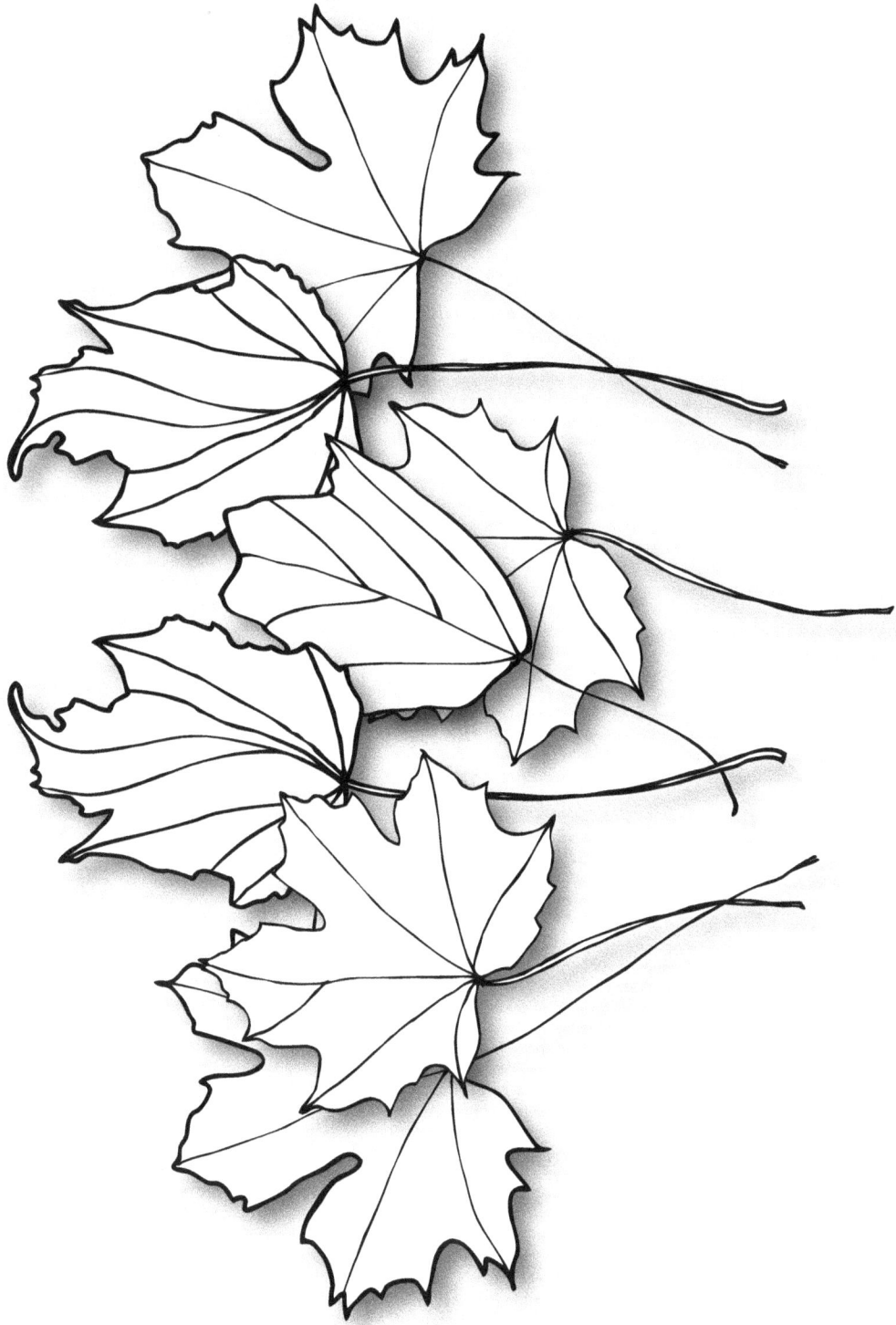

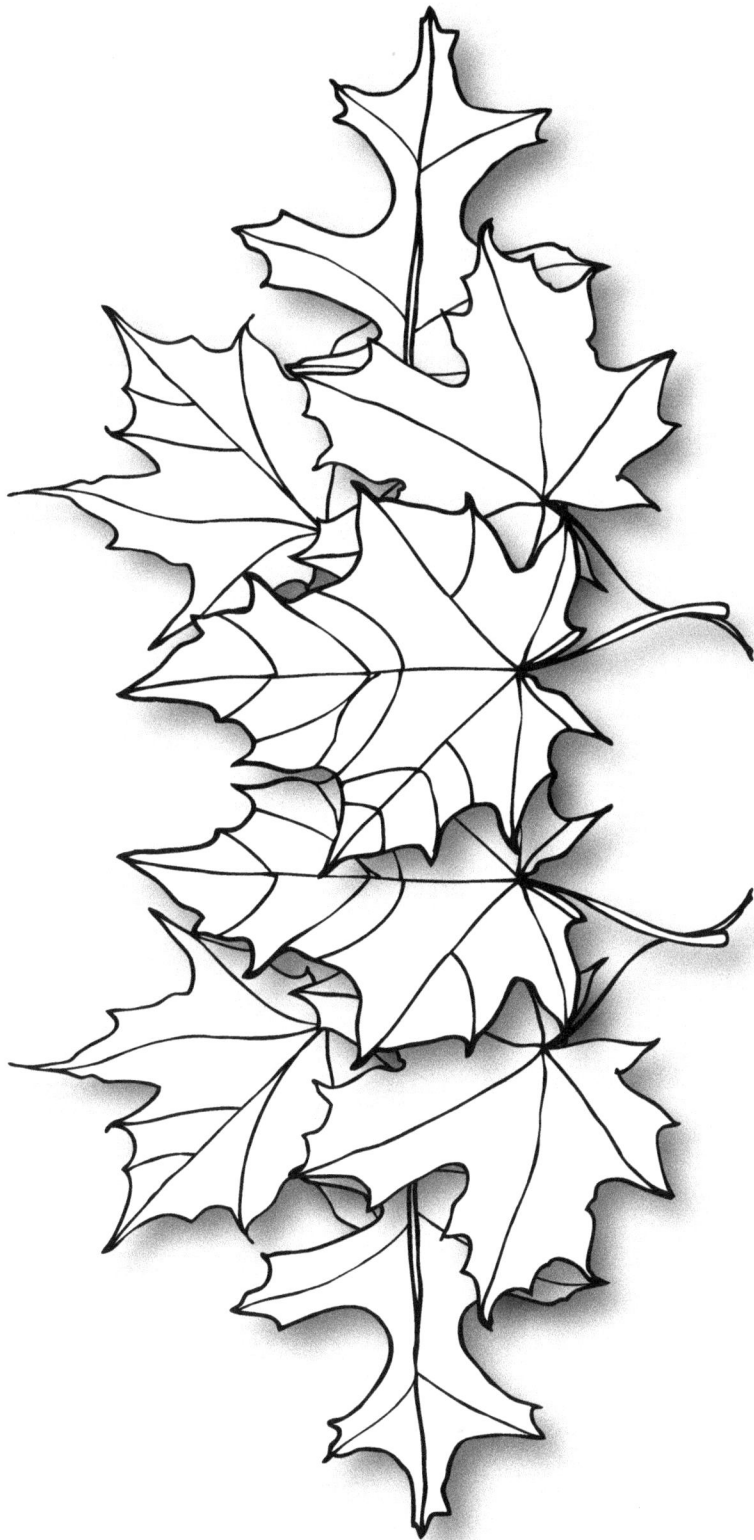

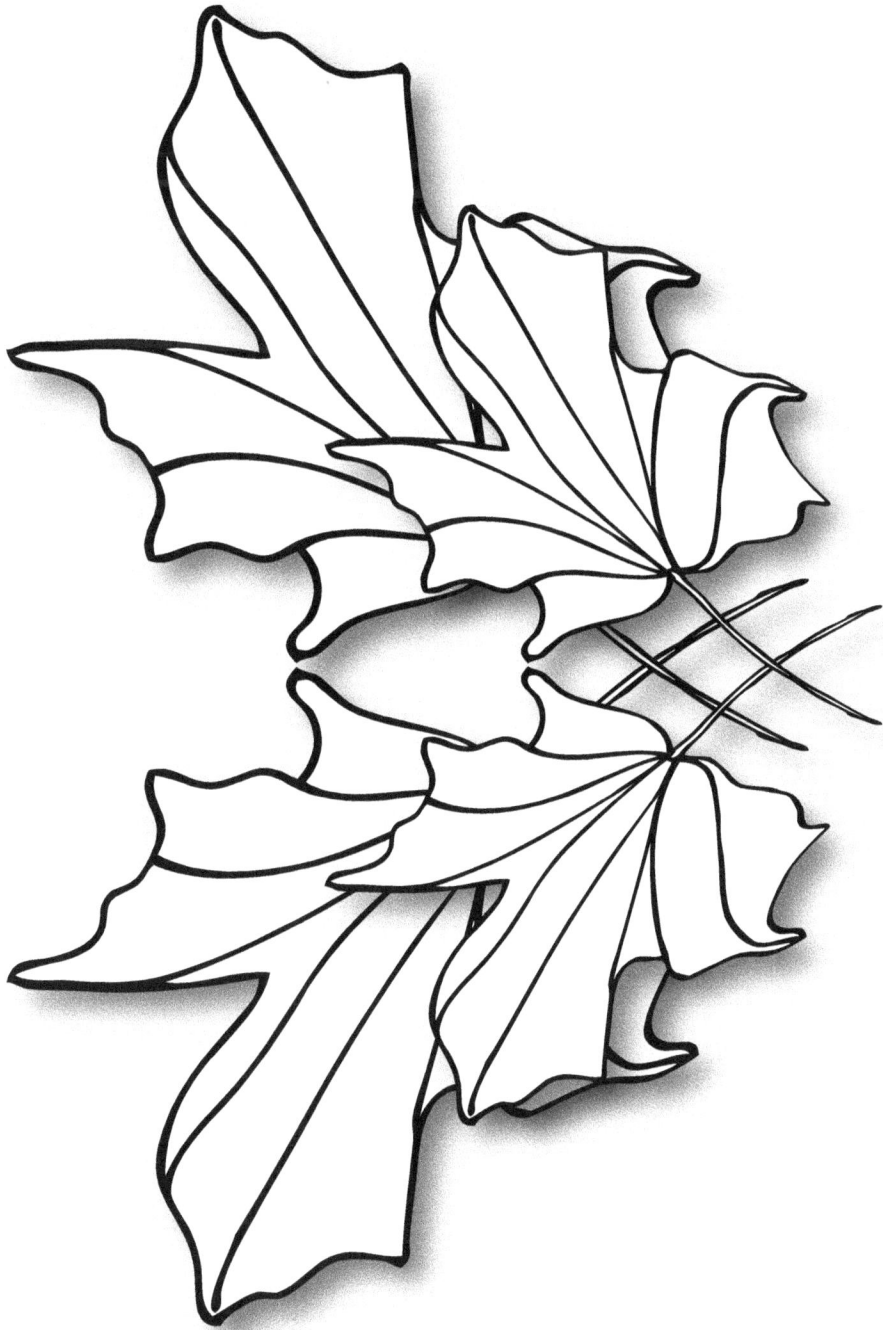

COLOR SWATCH TEST PAGE

Use this page to test and reference your colors

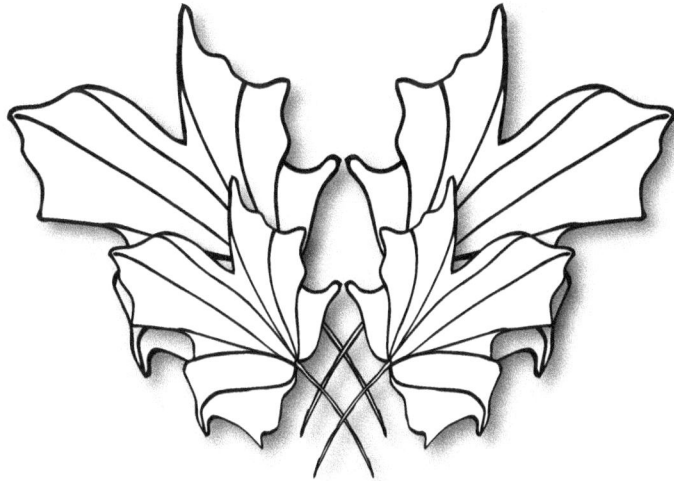

Fall Leaves Coloring Book
© 2015 Paula Parrish

To learn about current and upcoming books,
and view colored samples of the works contained herein,
please visit the author's website

www.lovely-leisure.com

www.ingramcontent.com/pod-product-compliance
Lightning Source LLC
Chambersburg PA
CBHW081226020426
42331CB00012B/3083